JUL 07 2015

*Through glimmering ice
and shimmering snow
On a frozen adventure,
here we go!*

*Glamorous jewelry
will make you look
like royalty.*

Princess power!

Share secrets with your friends when you all dress up like ice princesses together!

Design ice princess accessories with your own special flair!

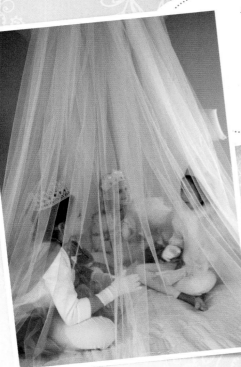

Have a yarn snowball fight inside where it's warm and cozy!

Once upon a time...

This illustration by an artist known only as H. L. M. shows the Norse mythological figure Skadi hunting in the snowy mountains. It appeared in a book of Norse tales published in 1901.

A Tale of the Magical Women of Ice and Snow

Fascination with women of the winter has been around for centuries! Before the Disney movie *Frozen* spellbound girls (and boys!) of all ages with winter magic and snow queens, there were folktales, stories, myths, and art dedicated to various wintry women, from princesses and queens to mythological figures. Read on to find out more about these amazing stories and all their similarities and differences throughout history.

"Royal" women of snow and ice with various wintry powers have been around for a very long time. There is Skadi, a Norse figure; Marzanna, a Baltic/Slavic mythological figure; the Cailleach Bheur, an Irish/Scottish mythological figure; and Snegurochka, a Russian snow maiden. Though each of these ladies has something in common—they are the ruler of or associated with winter—they also have their own unique characteristics.

Fascination with mysterious women of the winter has been around for centuries!

Skadi is a Norse mythological figure of winter and skiing who lives in the snow-covered mountains. Marzanna is a Baltic/Slavic figure of winter, and to this day it is a tradition in March in some areas of countries like Poland to destroy a figure of Marzanna to symbolize the end of winter. Then there is the Cailleach Bheur, an Irish/Scottish figure of winter, who appears as an old woman. Snegurochka is a Russian character whose story appears in several forms. In one, she is a girl made out of snow by a childless couple, and when she grows up and is playing with friends by jumping over a fire, she melts. In another story, she is Father Frost's daughter, and melts when she falls in love. Snegurochka later became part of the Russian New Year celebration, helping Father Frost give gifts to children.

This 1924 illustration of a scene from Hans Christian Andersen's tale "The Snow Queen" was done by Anne Anderson and shows young Kay being spirited away by the Snow Queen.

This 1899 painting by Russian artist Viktor Vasnetsov depicts Snegurochka, a snow girl from Russian folktales.

These mythological figures and characters lived for a long time in the minds and stories of their cultures. Then, in 1844, a Danish writer named Hans Christian Andersen created an original new tale of winter magic called "The Snow Queen," which appeared in his book *New Fairy Tales, First Volume, Second Collection*. Andersen wrote many novels, stories, and poems, and was one of the first writers responsible for bringing the fantastical aspects of the folktale genre into real literary works. Where writers like The Brothers Grimm collected oral tales (like the well-known stories of "Cinderella" and "Snow White") and wrote them down, Andersen actually created whole new tales that fit right in with the folktales already being told. Andersen was the writer of many favorite, famous tales that we know and love today, like "The Little Mermaid," "The Ugly Duckling," and "The Emperor's New Clothes."

GERDA BIDS FAREWELL TO THE LITTLE ROBBER GIRL.

"IT WAS THE SNOW QUEEN." (p. 5.)

These illustrations by Alfred Walter Bayes illustrated the story of "The Snow Queen" in an 1899 book of Hans Christian Andersen's fairy tales.

In this 1910 illustration by Margaret Tarrant, Kay meets the Snow Queen while sledding. The small illustrations around the edges of the image tell more of the story.

Though Andersen did not base his story "The Snow Queen" on any one mythological figure or folkloric tradition, the stories and magic of old peek through in his tale. In his story, a young boy named Kay gets a piece of a magic mirror in his heart that begins to slowly turn it to ice and enchant and change him. The magical Snow Queen kidnaps him and takes him to her grand ice and snow palace in the north. Kay's best friend, Gerda, goes looking for Kay and has many adventures on her journey, assisted by a crow, a princess, a robber girl, and a reindeer along the way. When Gerda finally finds Kay, she hugs him and cries on him, and this thaws the ice in his heart and turns him into himself again.

"The Snow Queen" and its characters have inspired many adaptations, including movies, TV shows, dance productions, plays, books, and even computer games. Some other popular and well-known characters seem to be inspired by the Snow Queen in Andersen's story, too, such as C. S. Lewis' character Jadis in *The Chronicles of Narnia*. Jadis, like the Snow Queen, has formidable wintry powers and kidnaps a young boy on her sled.

This book is great for anyone who wants to be a snow girl like Snegurochka or a magical queen like the Snow Queen herself.

It is interesting to see how different countries represent the same movie via their movie posters. Some countries show certain characters or scenes and some show none at all! These posters, in order, are from the United States, Poland, Russia, and South Korea.

Even fashion and styles got into the winter game! In the early twentieth century and even earlier, snowy fashions were a big hit during the winter season, and real-life snow "princesses" were featured in ads and magazines wearing capes and furry muffs.

Then, in 2013, Disney released a new film inspired by Andersen's story—with plenty of differences from the original plot—that took the world by storm: *Frozen*. People of all ages love the characters of Anna, Elsa, Olaf, Kristoff, Sven, and more. The movie helped

inspire tons of people to love all things snow, even in the middle of summer.

This book is the perfect place to get inspired to make your own winter wonderland of accessories, clothing, and toys, and is great for anyone who wants to be a snow girl like Snegurochka or a magical queen like the Snow Queen herself. So have fun becoming a part of history and grand stories with all these fun, cool crafts!

There are a lot of vintage photographs and illustrations dating from the late nineteenth and early twentieth centuries that show snowy girls cuddled up in fashionable muffs and clothes.

Meet a Real-Life Ice Princess

Meet Elsa! Or, rather, meet Angela Clayton, a talented 17-year-old sewer and *Frozen* fan from New York who applied her amazing skills to creating the best costume ever. Check out the Q&A below to learn more about Angela and how she made her great costume.

How did you get started in sewing and costume design?

I come from a family of quilters, so I learned the basics of sewing at a relatively young age. My original motivation for learning to sew actually came from costumery, since I wanted to bring my favorite fictional characters to life. For my first year of sewing, all my projects were based off of designs from series that I enjoyed. But I ended up loving the creative aspect so much that I started taking on more challenging projects, which eventually led to creating original and historical designs, which is now what I do almost exclusively.

What do you love about dressing up like Elsa?

There are a lot of things I love about it! For one thing, it's always fun dressing up as a character you respect or admire, which is definitely the case with Elsa. Seeing the finished project is really exciting and lovely too—that's usually my favorite part of wearing any of my creations. It makes me feel like all the effort and time was worth it! But for Elsa specifically, what I love is probably the thing that attracted me to the design in the first place, which is all the sparkles. The shimmer and glitter of freshly fallen snow was one of the things that made me want to make the costume. Wearing it around knowing that I achieved that makes me really happy.

What was the hardest part of the costume to make?

The cape was definitely the most challenging part of the whole costume. I glued down fifty snowflakes made with more than 150,000 rhinestones, so it was really repetitive and surprisingly mentally taxing. It took over two hundred hours to complete, and to make the process worse, I was using glue with really awful fumes and had to leave the windows of my room open for ventilation in the middle of winter! I worked on it in two hours shifts (or until my fingers went numb) several times a day for almost three months.

How did you do the hair and makeup?

I used a light foundation base (paired with a ton of concealer) and blush before starting on the eyes. I used a light purple eye shadow and darkened up the corners and creases with a gray, then finished it off with mascara and false eyelashes. I used a wig for the hair, so everything could be styled ahead of time. I made a simple braid up the back, then used a razor to cut the wispy fringe bits to the right length. The fringe was styled with hairspray, and I used pins to keep the strands in place while they set. It was finished off with two snowflake earrings I sewed into the braid!

What is your advice for someone who wants to dress up like Elsa?

Regardless of whether you are making or buying a costume, aim to wear something you are happy with. If that involves picking a design with personalized or unique details, go for it! Don't be afraid to make changes to the design that will make you like the end result more. For people making their own costumes, be patient! Saving a few hours of time is never worth sacrificing the quality of your costume, especially if you've already put a significant amount of time (or money) into making it. Details are important too—don't skimp on them.

Measuring the cape.

Gluing on the snowflakes.

The completed costume.

The Costume

...used more than 150,000 rhinestones.

...took more than 250 hours to make.

...took 3 months to create from start to finish.

...used 25 yards of fabric, including stretch mesh, silk chiffon, peachskin, cotton, and twill canvas.

...takes 40 minutes to put on, including the makeup.

Fantastic Party Ideas

Blogger and party planner Lilly Jimenez of I Heart Sugar Sugar in Miami (*www.iheartsugarsugar.com*) has thrown several mind-bogglingly awesome parties for her clients inspired by their love of the *Frozen* movie. With a lot of creativity and a great deal of vision, she made the snowy world of the movie come to life. She shares here just a sampling of her party ideas.

A glitzy snowflake ribbon decoration added glamor to all the chairs at this party.

This three-layer birthday cake made an amazing centerpiece for one lucky girl's birthday. Best of all, everything's edible, from the snowflakes to the tiara!

This glorious table setting features a fabric-covered backdrop decorated with delightful chipboard and paper snowflakes. The tasty treats on the table pop on the patterned tablecloth.

This fun-faced pillow was purchased in the perfect blue and then hand painted with fabric paint.

These yummy cookies came on a bed of snowy marshmallows.

TUTU DISPLAY BY I HEART SUGAR SUGAR, PHOTO BY STUDIO ONE SIX.

Tutus made great party favors for all the attendees at this party! These tutus even came with their own sparkly hangers.

DECORATION BY I HEART SUGAR SUGAR, PHOTO BY UNIQUE DESIGN STUDIOS.

At this event, partygoers were surrounded by icy fabric draping on the ceiling, wintery floral centerpieces, and passionately purple tablecloths.

This fabric and foam board table centerpiece stands out from all the ice and snow—in a good way!

SETUP BY I HEART SUGAR SUGAR, PHOTO BY UNIQUE DESIGN STUDIOS.

CAKE POPS BY O POPS BY ANGIE, PHOTO BY UNIQUE DESIGN STUDIOS.

A snowflake mold and fondant snowflakes on top made these rich chocolate brownies perfect for the party!

BROWNIES BY CAKES BY R.C., PHOTO BY UNIQUE DESIGN STUDIOS.

No one at this party could resist these cake pops, which were dipped in chocolate and covered in colored sanding sugar.

Superfan Gallery

Fans all over the world can't get enough of ice princesses. And as we researched ideas, it became clear that Disney's *Frozen* movie is the overwhelming inspiration for ice princess dress-up and crafting in all mediums. Tons of creative people have been busy crafting great clothes, gifts, food, art, and more. Check out some of the coolest examples of ice princess magic here!

Host a party in full-blown icy regalia like this princess!

Here's an example of a stunning over-the-top costume, including a delicately decorated dress and wig.

HAPPY BIRTHDAY

HAPPY 4th BIRTHDAY

Detailed ribbon adds a soft touch to these cupcakes.

This dessert table is true blue and tasty.

This ice-and-snow-themed party featured lots of blue, crystal, and glitter accents.

Thank You so much for celebrating with me! Juliet

Send guests home with snowflake favor boxes like these!

PARTY BY GWYNN WASSON (WWW.GWYNNWASSONDESIGNS.COM); PHOTOS BY MARCIE LENICK.

Fantastic cakes are a must-have for a show-stopping birthday party!

Snowflakes all over this cake make it shivery cold.

Get all your favorite characters on one cool cake!

Figurine toppers add a pop of color to an otherwise snowy blue cake.

Ribbon

Decorate anything with ribbon, and use it to fasten crowns and jewelry.

Scrapbook Paper

Sturdy paper is perfect for delicate, icy crowns.

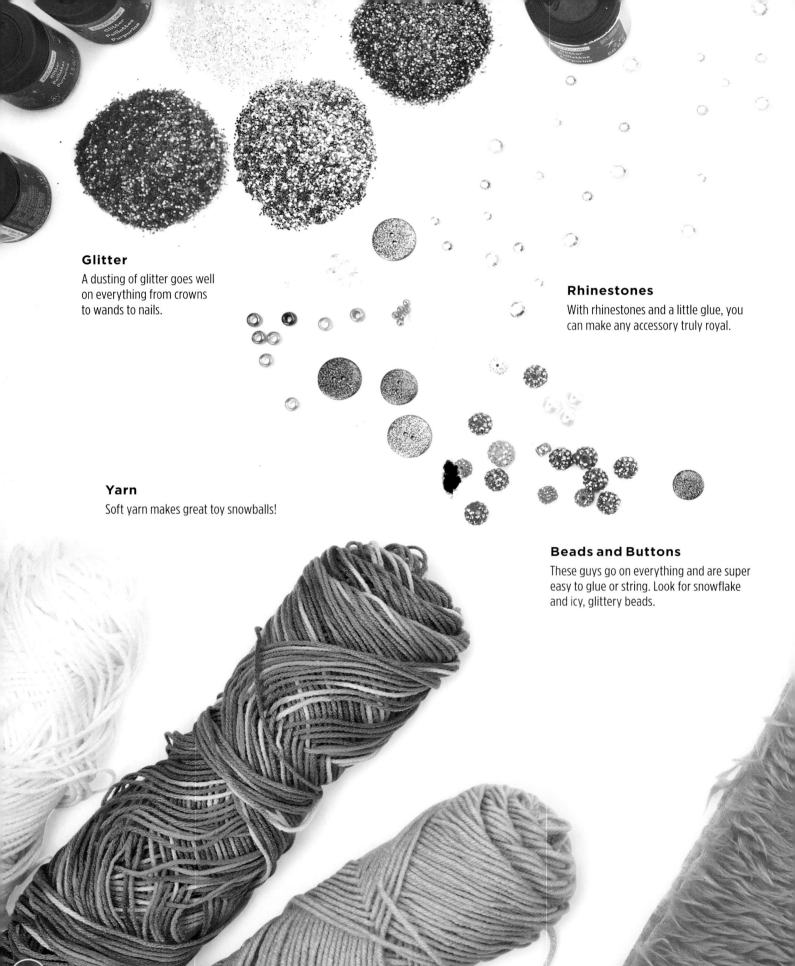

Glitter

A dusting of glitter goes well on everything from crowns to wands to nails.

Rhinestones

With rhinestones and a little glue, you can make any accessory truly royal.

Yarn

Soft yarn makes great toy snowballs!

Beads and Buttons

These guys go on everything and are super easy to glue or string. Look for snowflake and icy, glittery beads.

Paint

Jazz up wooden wands and other accessories with a pretty coat of paint.

Lace

Delicate and beautiful lace can be turned into crowns or used as embellishment.

Fabric

Faux fur is great for making warm winter accessories like the muff.

Princess Braids

Before you get into all your frozen finery, pin up your locks in a royal hairdo! Try one of these three beautiful ideas for a quick but stunning hairstyle.

Materials: brush, comb, rattail comb (for making parts and separating sections), hair ties, hair clips or clamps, bobby pins

Braided Headband Crown

1 Make a part from ear to ear to separate the hair into a front and a back section. Secure the back hair out of way, and then brush all the front hair over to one side.

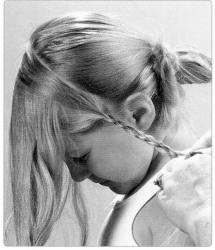

2 Make the first of three small braids using one third of the available front hair, the hair closest to the back of the head and the ear.

3 Make the other two small braids, one in the middle of the section and one in the front by the forehead.

4 Braid the three small braids together to form one big braid down the side of the head in front of the ear.

5 Fold the big braid back on itself, bringing it over and around the head like a headband. Secure it with a pin or clip behind the opposite ear.

6 Free the back section of hair and position it to make sure the loose hair hides where the braid is pinned. You may need to re-pin the braid or fluff the loose hair forward.

Princess Twist Bun

1 For this style, damp hair is best. Create a sharp side part, dividing the hair all the way down the back of the head. Secure the larger section of hair out of the way. On the unsecured side, select two small, evenly sized sections of hair from the front.

2 Twist the two sections around each other twice while pulling them toward the back of the head. It's best to stand behind and a little to the side of the head while working the twist.

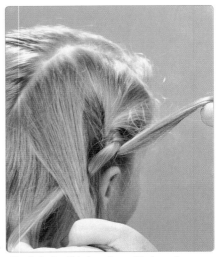

3 Select a third section of hair and combine it with the bottom (closest to head) section of hair already in your hand so you have two sections as you did in step 2. Twist the two sections around each other once. (You will only ever have two sections of hair to twist.)

4 Keep working all the way down the side of the head, combining new sections of loose hair with the two twist strands as you go. Don't combine the new section with the same twist strand twice in a row—this should happen naturally if you are twisting the hair only once every time.

5 Clamp the twist with a hair clamp at the base of the head to secure it temporarily. Repeat the twist on other side of the head, and then join the two twisted sides together in a ponytail at the back of the head, including any extra loose hair.

6 Twist the ponytail into a bun and secure it with a hair tie. Add bobby pins as needed along the twisted sides to secure them.

Side Fishtail

1 For this braid, damp to wet hair is best. Brush all the hair to one side of the head.

2 Select two evenly sized sections of hair, one from the front and one from the back.

3 Cross the back section over the front section. Hold those two sections separate in one hand, and grab a new section from the front.

4 Combine the new section with the top section (which was originally the back section), as shown. Then grab a new section from the back and combine it with the bottom section (which was originally the front section).

5 Cross the back section over the front section again, as you did in step 3, and keep repeating the pattern: add to each section, and then cross the back over the front.

6 Fasten the braid with a hair tie. If the hair is layered, simply stop at the shortest layer and fasten the braid there.

Glamorous Gloves

Glam it up with elbow-length embellished gloves to keep you warm and stylish in winter. You can choose to decorate your gloves with anything from paint to rhinestones to pom-poms, or add ribbon for a magical effect!

Materials: pair of gloves, embellishments like pom-poms, rhinestones, puffy fabric paint, or ribbon as needed

Puff Paint

Trace the glove swirl design (page 63) onto the gloves very lightly with a thin pencil line, or slide the pattern inside the glove if you can see the pattern through the fabric. Trace over the pattern lines with puff paint.

Ribbon Surprise

Cut 10 long pieces of ribbon for each glove. Hot glue them together at one end, and then hot glue one group of ribbon to the palm of each glove. To show off your icy powers, gather the ribbon up in your hands and throw!

Rhinestone

Trace the glove swirl design (page 63) onto the gloves very lightly with tiny pencil dots, or slide the pattern inside the glove if you can see the pattern through the fabric. Use fabric glue to add a rhinestone over each dot.

Pom-Pom
Use hot glue to add pom-poms all around the opening of both gloves. Add a single large pom-pom to a finger of one glove as a ring. Make a circle of tiny pom-poms around a finger on the other glove as a ring.

Royal Crowns

What's a queen without a crown? Make yours out of your favorite material, whether that's felt, foam, or glitter paper. Or make an even fancier, unique crown with lace or faux sparkle branches. What's your royal style?

Materials for Lace Crown: piece of crocheted lace, fabric stiffener, spray paint or fabric paint, embellishments like glitter or rhinestones as desired

Glitter Paper

Cut out the cutout crown pattern (page 60) either as a solid outline or with all the cutouts from glitter paper. (If you want to do the cutouts, use a craft knife and get an adult's help.)

Foam

Cut out the simple crown pattern (page 59) from foam. Decorate the crown with big faux gems and rhinestones.

Felt

Cut out two copies of the snowflake crown pattern (page 58), including one copy of the snowflakes, from felt. Glue the two crown pieces together to make a thick piece of felt, add the snowflakes to the front, and glue on pom-poms and beads.

Ice Sparkle Branches

Wrap semi-pliable sparkle branches into a circular crown shape and tie the ends together with ribbon. Make the crown extra secure by wrapping some thin silver wire around it at a different spot than the ribbon.

Lace

1 Measure and cut a piece of lace to fit around your head plus 2" (5cm). Wrap the lace around a cylindrical form like a large coffee can and secure it temporarily with tape. Spray the lace with fabric stiffener following the manufacturer's directions.

2 Once the lace is dry, remove it from the form. You can now decorate it further: try painting it with glitter fabric paint as shown here, or add snowflakes, gems, or other decorations.

3 Permanently secure the crown closed with hot glue, overlapping the ends by 1" (2.5cm) to use up the extra 2" (5cm) of length added in step 1.

Shimmering Magic Wands

Sometimes ice princesses need to channel their magical powers through a tool like a wand. That's okay, though, because wands make stunning accessories that let everyone know who's in charge! Whatever wand you choose, wave it responsibly!

Materials for Tulle Pouf Wand: spools of 6" (15cm)-wide tulle, embroidery or sewing thread, wooden dowel, ribbon

Tulle Pouf

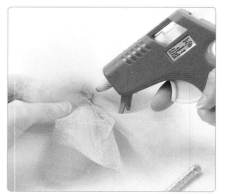

1 Cut 20–40 tulle rectangles about 4" x 6" (10 x 15cm) from a spool of tulle. If your tulle is not exactly 6" (15cm) wide, just cut rectangles that are 4" (10cm) by the width of your tulle.

2 Divide the rectangles into two even piles. Use thread to tie a knot tightly around the center of each pile, forming a bow with the tulle. Lay one tied pile on top of the other so they are perpendicular to one another and the tulle forms a circle. Tie the two piles together.

3 Separate all the layers of tulle to make the poufy sphere shape. Wrap ribbon around a dowel, gluing it in place as you go, to make a decorative wand handle. Use hot glue to attach the handle to the pouf.

Felt

Trace and cut out two copies of the snowflake wand pattern (page 61) from felt and add pom-poms. Sandwich the dowel between the two circles and secure everything in place with hot glue. Then use fabric glue to add beads to the snowflakes and edges.

Wood Cutout

Paint a wooden dowel and a wooden cutout white. Hot glue the dowel to the cutout, and then add small rhinestones to the head of the wand.

Glitter Paper

Cut out two copies of the cutout wand pattern (page 61) either as a solid outline or with all the cutouts. (Use a craft knife and get an adult's help to do the cutouts.) Hot glue the pieces around a dowel.

Foam

Cut out two copies of the star wand pattern (page 61), including the big star and the mini star, from foam. Use hot glue to secure the foam pieces around a dowel. Add a big gem to the center.

Winter Wonder Cape

The one essential accessory for any ice princess is a luxurious winter cape! This cape might not keep you too warm, but it sure does dazzle the eye and make you look like you're ready to rule. Choose a fur or a ribbon tie for a custom look.

Materials: 3 yd. (3m) tulle, at least 72" (180cm) of 1" (2.5cm)-wide sparkle ribbon, sewing thread, sewing machine, pins

1 Cut a 5' x 9' (150 x 275cm) piece of tulle. You can go shorter or longer than 9' (275cm) if you want to make a shorter or longer cape.

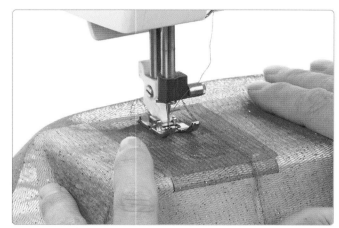

2 Fold the tulle in half so that it forms a double layered piece that is 5' x 4.5' (150 x 135cm). Sew two parallel lines of very long straight stiches (without backstitching) along the open 5' (150cm) edge, stitching one line 3" (8cm) from the edge and the second line 3½" (9cm) from the edge.

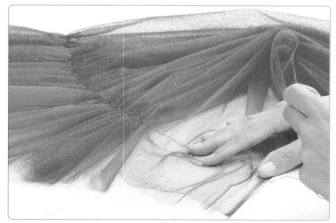

3 Tie the threads at one end together and gently pull on the bobbin threads at the other end, sliding the tulle along the threads to gather it. Gather the tulle until the edge measures about 12" (30cm) wide, making the gathers as even as possible. Knot the loose threads and machine sew the edge to hold the gathers in place.

4 Center and pin about 72" (180cm) or longer of 1" (2.5cm)-wide ribbon to the neckline, over the rows of gathering stitches. Stitch along each long edge of the ribbon to secure it to the tulle at the neckline.

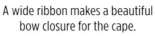
A wide ribbon makes a beautiful bow closure for the cape.

No-Sew Cape: *Don't feel like sewing? That's okay! Fold the tulle as described in step 2, and then use double-sided tape to temporarily hold it together. Cut about 8–10 vertical slices along the neckline of the cape, starting the slits about 3" (8cm) down from the edge, then thread the long ribbon through. Scrunch up the tulle along the ribbon, and you're good to go!*

Combining a glittery crown with glittery tulle will make you sparkle with every step you take!

A fuzzy fur collar will keep your neck cozy in the cool winds of winter.

Faux Fur Option: *If you want to make an extra-luxurious cape, use a strip of faux fur or feathers as a tie instead of a ribbon!*

Snowspray Tulle Tutu

Dance through the snow in this fun skirt! The simple construction makes it a cinch to craft, but the final effect is just stunning. You and your friends can enjoy wearing this tutu at all sorts of princess events!

Materials: spools of 6" (15cm)-wide tulle in 3 colors, sturdy ribbon or cord for belt

1 Measure the circumference of your waist and add 24" (60cm). Cut a piece of wide, sturdy ribbon to that length to use as the tutu belt.

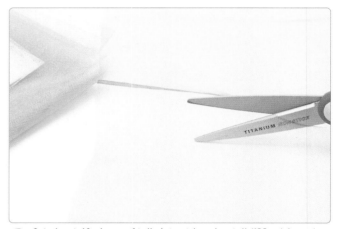

2 Cut about 40 pieces of tulle into strips about 4' (122cm) long (or twice as long as you want the tutu to be) and about 6" (15cm) wide. (Many tulle spools are 6" [15cm] wide.) You can also cut strips from yards of tulle, as shown in the photo.

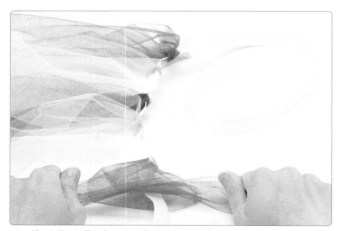

3 Knot the tulle pieces at their center points around the ribbon in an alternating color pattern. Mix it up: knot some pieces singly, and knot other pieces two at a time.

4 Slide the knots around the ribbon so they are all evenly spaced along the middle portion. Leave 12" (30cm) at each end of the ribbon free to use as the tie. Then try on the tutu and tie it closed!

Cuddly Muff & Stole

When heading into a snowstorm or just a chilly winter's day, you'll want to make sure you take this soft matching muff and stole. The muff will keep your hands toasty, while the stole wraps securely around your neck like a scarf. Get an adult's help to sew these projects.

Materials for Muff or Stole: ½ yd. (½m) blue faux fur fabric, ½ yd. (½m) white faux fur fabric (muff only), sewing thread, sewing machine, pins

No Worries: *A universal needle will work fine to sew through your average faux fur fabric.*

The stole requires such simple sewing that you'll be cozily wearing it in no time!

Make your muff in blue and white to match the rest of your ice princess outfit.

Muff

Most faux fur is machine washable, so you can use your muff all the time and clean it in a jiffy before your next snowy adventure!

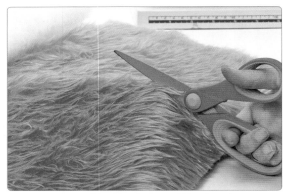

1 Cut a 12" x 9" (30 x 23cm) piece of blue faux fur fabric and a 12" x 14" (30 x 35cm) piece of white faux fur fabric.

2 With right sides facing, align two of the 12" (30cm) edges and pin along that edge. Stitch along the pinned edge using a ½" (1.5cm) seam allowance. Align and pin the remaining 12" (30cm) edges together and stitch as before. This will form a tube of fabric as shown.

3 Turn the tube right side out and lay it flat with the blue fabric on top in the center. Adjust the tube as needed so the white fabric on either side of the blue is even. Then fold the piece in half lengthwise with the blue fabric hidden from view in the middle as shown. Stitch along the open edge using a ½" (1.5cm) seam allowance.

4 Turn the piece right side out and trim away any loose thread ends.

1 Cut a 12" x 30" (30 x 75cm) piece of blue faux fur fabric.

The stole is so soft you'll never want to take it off!

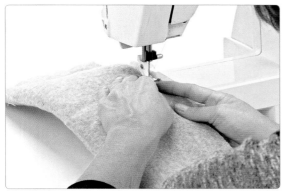

2 Fold the fabric in half lengthwise with right sides facing and pin along all the open edges to create a long tube. Using a ½" (1.5cm) seam allowance, stitch along one short edge (stitching away from the fold), turn the corner, and continue stitching until you are halfway along the long edge, then stop.

3 After leaving about a 6" (15cm) opening for turning, continue stitching along the long edge, turn the corner, and stitch along the remaining short edge.

4 Use the opening you left for turning to turn the piece right side out. Hand stitch the opening closed with a ladder stitch.

Pin It: *Secure your stole around your neck with a cute snowflake pin or other favorite pin.*

Frosted Nail Art

Everyone has some nail polish lying around the house, and it doesn't take much to turn your nails into beautiful works of art! Whether you like a simple ombré color change or want to go all out with glitter, there's a style here for you to try.

Materials: nail polish in assorted colors, nail polish remover, toothpicks, glitter and rhinestones as needed

Snowflake

Paint your nails a deep winter night blue and let the polish dry. Then add little snow dots and a big snowflake using a toothpick dabbed in white polish.

Glitter

Paint your nails with a layer of white or silver polish, and, while the polish is still wet, sprinkle glitter onto the nails. Let the polish dry. Then add a clear topcoat and sprinkle more glitter onto the new wet coat. Let the polish dry again, and then add one or two more clear topcoats.

Ombré

Paint each nail on both hands in an increasingly dark shade of purple. If you want, you can even mix small amounts of white and purple on a disposable plate to make custom colors.

Rhinestone

Paint your nails light blue and wait for the polish to dry. Then adhere tiny rhinestones to your nails. Be sure to use glue that's specially made for use on nails if you are painting your real nails instead of false ones.

Ice Crystal Shoes

Everywhere you go, people will stop and stare at your dazzling shoes! The glittery heart pattern is super cute, and the shoes look like they cost you a million bucks. Your secret? You made them yourself!

Materials: sneakers, rhinestones in varying shades of blue and white, fabric or super glue

1 Using a pencil or anything else that won't leave a strong mark, draw a half heart shoe design (as shown) on the inside edge of one shoe. Repeat on the other shoe and put both shoes together to make sure they match up.

2 Glue your darkest rhinestones onto each shoe to fill the center heart area. You can use a pair of tweezers to carefully place each stone if you like.

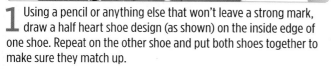

3 Outline the center area with white rhinestones. Keep adding additional bands of color, moving outward and alternating lighter shades of blue and white, until you reach the outer edge of the pattern. Sprinkle the smallest rhinestones around the edges of the heart shape.

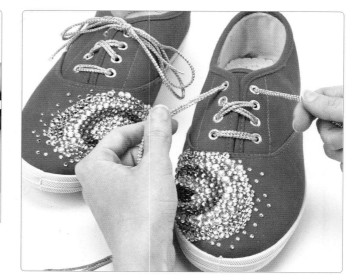

4 Lace up the shoes in your favorite lacing pattern with fun cord or shoelaces.

Snowy Hair Accessories

Adorn your lovely princess locks with these accessories for any hair texture or length! Clip a fun barrette in for a pop of color, or put on a braided headband to get into character as a real snow queen.

Materials: plain headband or barrette bases, embellishments like jewelry wire, beads, yarn, or buttons as needed

Try using glamorous faux pearl beads to make this headband.

Beaded Headband

Cut a piece of beading wire at least 80" (200cm) long. Wrap one end of the wire securely around one end of the headband. Then string as many beads as you want in one row onto the wire. Settle the first row of beads against the headband, and tightly wrap the wire around the headband to hold them in place. Repeat to add as many rows of beads as you'd like.

Button Collage Barrette

Use hot glue to layer sparkly buttons on top of one another one at a time to create a collage look. When you're satisfied with the button collage, hot glue it to a barrette base.

Statement Snowflake Barrette

Cut out the pieces of the snowflake barrette pattern (page 62) from felt. Glue the pieces together in layers, going from the largest to the smallest. Then hot glue the layered snowflake to a barrette.

Braid Headband

Cut 30 strands of white yarn that are 60" (150cm) long. Tie all 30 strands together tightly onto one end of a headband base with a small piece of yarn. Divide the strands into 3 groups of 10 strands each. Braid the 3 groups together in a basic braid and tie off with ribbon or yarn. Hot glue the braid onto the headband.

Icy Jewels

Whether you want to make a show-stopping jewelry set, a classy occasion necklace, or a super-cool leather cuff, there's an idea here for you. Some of the trickier techniques might require an adult's help, but the end results will blow your mind!

Materials for Glitzy Jewelry Set: 48" (120cm) cord for necklace, 13" (33cm) cord for bracelet, 40" (100cm) contrasting cord for ties, assorted beads, ring blank

Glitzy Jewelry Set

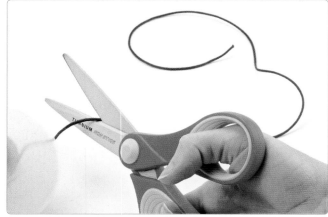

1 To make the necklace, cut two pieces of your chosen cord, one 22" (56cm) long and one 26" (66cm) long. To make the bracelet, cut a piece of cord that is the circumference of your wrist plus about 6" (15cm).

2 On one end of each piece of cord, knot a loop that is about the circumference of your finger—put your finger through the loop as you tighten the knot. Make sure the knot is secure before proceeding.

3 Thread beads onto the cords in the desired pattern. When you have finished beading, knot the loose ends of the cords the same way you did the first ends, making a loop.

4 Cut two pieces of your chosen tie cord in about 10" (25cm) lengths. Knot one end of each tie cord onto both loops at one end of the necklace (or onto one loop at one end of the bracelet). Tie the cords together to wear the piece.

Making the Ring: *The matching ring takes just a minute to make. Glue a button and a bead to a ring blank with hot glue, and you're done!*

Classy Necklace

Materials for Classy Necklace: 16" (40cm) beading wire, jewelry findings (clasp, 2 jump rings or split rings, 2 crimp beads), assorted beads, straight nose jewelry pliers

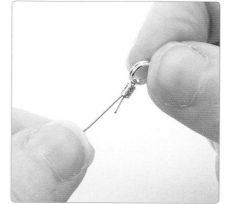

1 Lay out your design on a towel to make sure it's symmetrical and you have all the beads that you need in the correct order.

2 String a jump ring or split ring onto one end of a 16" (40cm) length of beading wire and secure it in place by pinching a crimp bead with pliers. Then string the beads. (Look online for more tips on how to work with crimp beads and jump rings.)

3 After you are done beading, secure the other end of the necklace with another crimp bead and jump ring or split ring, and then add the clasp.

Leather Princess Cuff

Materials for Leather Princess Cuff: 8" (20cm) strip of colored leather about 2" (5cm) wide, 12" (30cm) cord, leather punch or hammer and awl, snowflake sticker

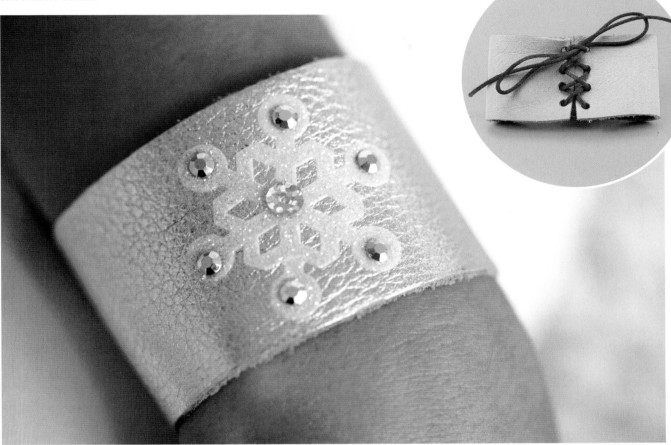

1 Cut a piece from a 2" (5cm)-wide colored leather strip about ½" (1.5cm) longer than the circumference of your wrist. Fold the strip in half, bringing the short ends together, and use a leather punch to punch evenly spaced holes through both short ends.

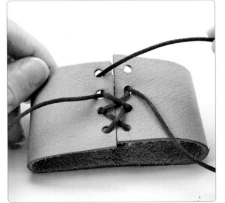

2 Cut a long piece of your chosen cord— at least 12" (30cm)—and thread it through the holes to lace up the cuff. Tie the ends together in a bow.

3 Put a snowflake sticker or other embellishment on the front of the cuff.

Winter Waterfall Canopy

Make your bedroom into a royal chamber by hanging this glamorous canopy from the ceiling. The beautiful multicolored drapes will add fun and zest to your already awesome personal space. It takes a lot of fabric, but it's totally worth it!

Materials: 24 yd. (24m) tulle in 3 colors (8 yd. [8m] each color), 14" (35cm)-diameter wooden embroidery hoop, white spray paint, white ribbon

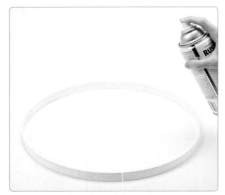

1 Disassemble the 14" (35cm)-diameter embroidery hoop into two pieces. Spray paint one piece white. Save the remaining piece for a second canopy or another craft project.

2 Cut four 4 yd. (4m)-long panels of each color of tulle where the final width of each panel is at least 24" (60cm). Tulle is often sold in a double layer, so you can do this by cutting each 8 yd. (8m) piece of tulle in half and then cutting those pieces in half lengthwise. For the super-thick canopy shown, use double the tulle: 16 yd. (16m) per color.

3 Knot one end of each panel around the painted embroidery hoop in an alternating color pattern, leaving some tulle extended above each knot at the top to create a crown.

4 Tie four lengths of ribbon onto the hoop at even intervals, and then tie the loose ends of all the ribbons together at the top. Install a hook in the ceiling where you want the canopy to hang, and use the ribbons to suspend it. Adjust the ribbon lengths as necessary to make sure the hoop hangs evenly.

Yarn Snowballs

Whenever you're bored, just sit down and make some soft, fuzzy snowballs that will never melt. You'll soon have enough for an indoor snowball fight with your friends in any season!

Materials: skeins of yarn in white, blue, purple, and multicolor

Front

Back

1 Cut a 12" (30cm) piece of yarn for a tie and set it aside. You'll need anywhere from 28' (860cm) to 70' (2m) of yarn per snowball. Wrap the yarn (right off the skein) around the widest part of your hand, snugly and evenly. When you've wrapped enough, cut the yarn free from the skein.

2 Remove the "doughnut" from your hand, but keep hold of the hole. Lay the tie yarn across the middle of the doughnut and wrap each end around the back and up through the center hole toward you. Cross the strands and wrap the two ends around to the back of the doughnut again. Tie the strands together very tightly with a knot to hold the donut in place.

3 Cut all the yarn loops on the doughnut into individual strands. Push your scissors through a few loops at a time and pull them up to make sure you cut the loops at the very top.

4 Trim the strands even all around the snowball to make it spherical. The shorter you cut the strands, the firmer and thicker the snowball will be.

Hanging Snowballs:
If you want to hang your snowball, it's really easy. After you tie the doughnut in step 2, but before you start cutting the loops in step 3, just cut a long piece of yarn and tie it around the doughnut. Be careful not to cut it when cutting the loops!

Patterns

All patterns appear at 100%.

Snowflake Crown

Project on page 30.

Simple Crown

Project on page 30.

Digital Bonus Patterns Available!

Scan the code above with your smart phone or visit **www.d-originals.com/iceprincesscrafts** to download printable patterns.

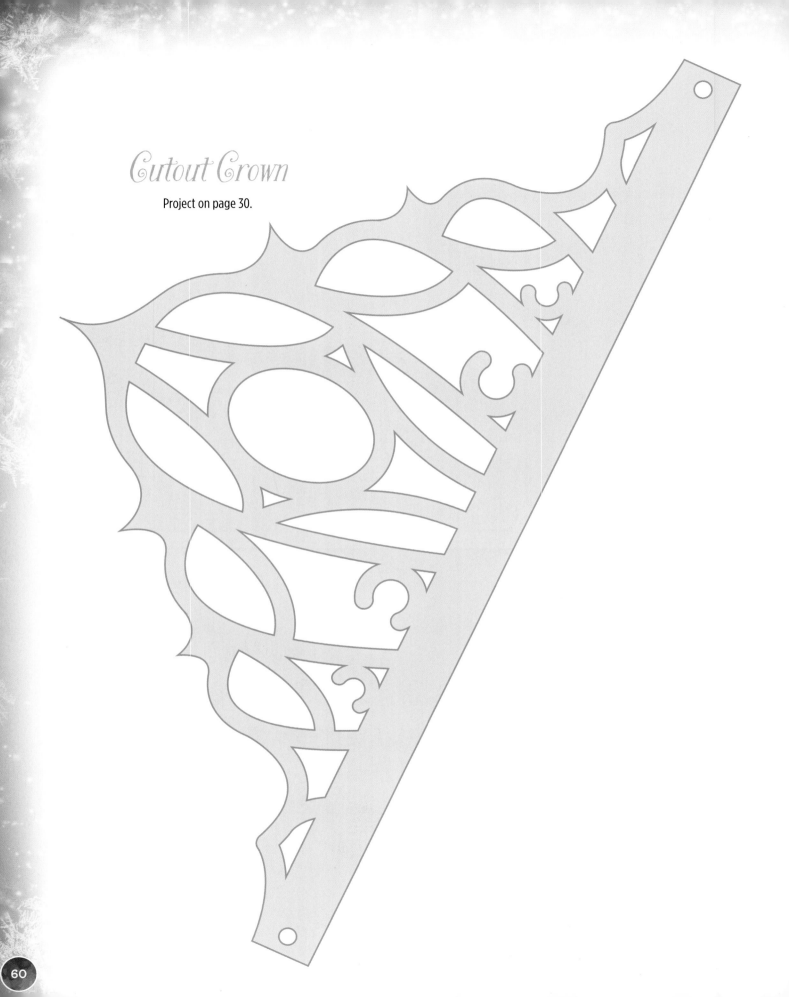

Cutout Crown

Project on page 30.

Star Wand

Project on page 32.

Cutout Wand

Project on page 32.

Snowflake Wand

Project on page 32.

Snowflake Barrette
Project on page 48.

Glove Swirl Design

Project on page 28.

Index

Note: Page numbers in *italics* indicate projects and related patterns.

The snow has stopped
The day is done
Being a princess
Has sure been fun!